THE INGLIS LECTURE

1959

INGLIS LECTURES
IN SECONDARY EDUCATION

The Revolutionary Transformation
of the American High School

The Revolutionary Transformation of the American High School

JAMES BRYANT CONANT

CAMBRIDGE, MASSACHUSETTS

HARVARD UNIVERSITY PRESS

1959

THE INGLIS LECTURESHIP

To honor the memory of Alexander Inglis, 1879–1924, his friends and colleagues gave to the Graduate School of Education, Harvard University, a fund for the maintenance of a Lectureship in Secondary Education. To the study of problems in this field Professor Inglis devoted his professional career, leaving as a precious heritage to his co-workers the example of his industry, intellectual integrity, human sympathy, and social vision. It is the purpose of the Lectureship to perpetuate the spirit of his labors and contribute to the solution of problems in the field of his interest. The lectures on this foundation are published annually by the School.

The Revolutionary Transformation
of the American High School

THE GREAT PHILOSOPHERS from Plato to Whitehead have written about the aims of education. Their writings have profoundly influenced the way men and women have thought about the problems of bringing up children. Their discussions of the nature of knowledge and the way knowledge is passed on from one generation to another have provided countless teachers with a set of ideas basic to their profession. Yet it is quite evident to anyone who reads books and articles about schools and colleges that when lesser lights have attempted to define education, the results more often than not have been neither novel nor illuminating. Over the years I have wrestled with definitions and struggled with chains of logical reasoning; I have been guilty of my share of educational banalities. As a consequence, I must confess to an increasing distrust of the use of the deductive method of thinking about questions confronting teachers. When someone writes or says that what we need today in the United States is to decide first what we mean by the word "education," a sense of distasteful weariness overtakes me. I feel as though I were starting to see a badly scratched film of a poor movie for the second or third time. In such moods, I am ready to define education as what goes on in schools and colleges. And I submit that, nine times out of ten, such a formulation at least outlines the area of debate, though I realize full well there is always someone present in the audience to rise to a point of order and at some length explain that the speaker has mistaken schooling for education.

Tonight I am going to talk about the revolution in American secondary education which has taken place in my lifetime. I have in mind the transformation of the public high schools which occurred between, let us say, 1905 and 1930. My introductory remarks will have made clear the spirit in which I ask you to join with me in analyzing this bit of recent history. As to the relevance of my remarks to the recent furor about public schools generated by two Sputniks, I must leave the verdict to this audience. According to my own interpretation of the last fifty years, the American public between 1930 and 1945 was so concerned with first a depression and then a global war that few laymen fully realized that a revolutionary transformation of the schools had just occurred. Only after the post-war adjustment had been made did any large number of articulate Americans wake up to what had happened. And as often is the case with those suddenly awakened from a deep sleep, the first exclamations were not too closely related to the actual situation.

In 1905 something like a third of the children who first enrolled in grade one entered a high school (grade nine). Only about nine percent of an age group graduated from high school, and only four or five percent of an age group entered college. In 1930, instead of only a third of the youth entering high school, well over three-quarters were registered in the ninth grade; instead of nine percent graduating, almost forty-five percent of an age group finished high school; and the college entries had risen from five percent of an age group to about fifteen percent. It is interesting to note that while the percentage attending college increased, the percentage of high school graduates going on for further education declined because of the greater increase in high school enrollment.

In 1905, the curriculum of almost all public high schools was academic. The country over, half the pupils in grades nine to twelve were studying Latin. Few if any schools, except manual training schools, were offering courses involving senior shopwork for boys; few girls were studying, at taxpayers' expense, stenography, domestic economy, or bookkeeping; little, if any, time was devoted to art and music. By 1930 the widely comprehensive high school was to be found in many sections of the country. Boys and girls were spending as much as half their time in grades eleven and twelve on courses designed to develop skills marketable on graduation; the art and music departments were expanding rapidly; Latin was disappearing from the curriculum except for a two-year course. Institutions of higher education, both private and public, were enrolling students whose only academic credential was a high school diploma, and by 1930 this often meant the graduate had a minimum exposure to those academic subjects considered essential twenty-five years before.

How and why did the revolutionary change occur? To read some accounts, one would think that a band of professors of education had decided that for the future well-being of our society, it was essential that all American youth stay in school full time through grade twelve. Therefore, they enlisted the teachers, as in a crusade, and persuaded the state legislators to raise the age of compulsory attendance to force the boys and girls to stay in school. They then proceeded to focus attention on education for citizenship and understanding the ways of democracy. The high school curriculum was revolutionized to correspond to this new approach, and a host of elective courses was provided to take care of the wide spectrum of abilities and interests in the high school population, which was now to include *all* the youth of a city, town, or district. According to those who see the revolution in the way I have just described, John Dewey's *School and Society*, first published in 1899, and his *Democracy and Education*, published in 1916, were the inspiration and guide for the educational crusade.

Quite a different account might run as follows: The transformation in methods of production which we talk so much about today had already started in the first decade of this century. Apprentice training, characteristic of Europe, was disappearing. The land-grant colleges were making the farmers conscious that going to college might have practical value, and, therefore, it was worth while for a boy to finish high school in order to get to college. A vigorous humanitarian movement to abolish child labor was getting under way; Congress in 1916 passed a law prohibiting child labor. Though the federal law was declared unconstitutional, the momentum of the movement to abolish child labor was far from lost.

State laws were passed regulating the employment of young people. A demand for vocational education grew rapidly; it was backed by factory owners, farmers, and labor leaders, and resulted in the passage of the Smith-Hughes Act in 1917, which appropriates federal funds for vocational education. These social, economic, and legal changes, taken together with an attitude of some labor leaders who were anxious to restrict rather than expand the number of applicants for jobs, forced many young people to stay in school. A generation earlier, the same type of youngster would have gone to work at fourteen or even younger. As a consequence, from 1905 to 1930 the schools from grades six to twelve were filling up with types of pupils different from those the teachers had known before. The teachers appealed to the professors in the teachers' colleges for help. Their cries of distress were answered by such writings as John Dewey's volume of 1916 and the *Cardinal Principles of Secondary Education*, published in 1918 by a Commission of the National Education Association. In short, according to this second view, it was the change in the employment picture which forced parents to keep their children in school, irrespective of their academic talent and their desire to go to college. This change in the nature of the high school population, in turn, forced the school administrators, teachers, and educational theoreticians to accommodate the high schools to the new order.

I have purposely sketched two extreme interpretations of an educational transformation. The first puts the educators triumphantly in the driver's seat; the second depicts them as conscientious public servants trying to do their best to solve problems not of their own making. One may be quick to say that the truth lies somewhere in between these two extremes and, furthermore, that an analysis of this past episode in American education is of interest only to historians. But, as to this last point, I would disagree. The nature of the transformation of the high school bears directly on the current discussion of the shortcomings of American public secondary education — the discussion which took such a violent emotional turn after the Russian success with rockets in the fall of 1957. I have read accounts of the revolution in American education which come very close to the interpretation I first put forward. In such accounts, the raising of the school-leaving age is the one legal sanction, so to speak, which the reforming educators required to forward their ambitions toward universal education of American youth. And more than one layman has accepted at face value the educators' account of the revolution which the educators claim was theirs. Some laymen, perhaps the great majority, have applauded, but in recent years some have had grave misgivings. Not a few have said: "If the professionals can persuade the legislators to raise the school-leaving age, why can't some of us get together and lower it?" Continuing the argument, such laymen are apt to say: "There are a lot of boys and girls in high school today who have no business being there; they haven't the interest or ability to benefit from what a school ought to be concerned with, namely, training and nourishing the mind. Let's change the laws on compulsory school attendance and get back to where we were in the first decade of this century."

Some such statements have been made to me more than once in the last two years. Implicit in the point of view thus expressed is the notion that the revolutionary transformation of the high school was a social change which, like prohibition, could be reversed. One pressure group succeeded in amending the Constitution to prohibit the sale of liquor, and a second succeeded later in nullifying this amendment by the adoption of still another. Thus a new social situation, which in the 1920's appeared to many to be permanent, turned out to be only temporary. If one clock, prohibition, could be turned back, why not another, namely, education; so argued privately some educational counter-revolutionists.

Is the change in the educational pattern which occurred between 1905 and 1930 comparable to the change brought about by the prohibition amendment, or is it more like the change in our methods of transportation which occurred in about the same period of time? Both transformations — the one affecting the drinking habits of the American public, the other the habits of locomotion — were the result of free decisions. That is to say, no dictator, no occupying power, promulgated decrees or put the force of the state to work to modify our habits. Clearly, the first change — prohibition — could be reversed by a change of law, but equally clearly the second cannot; a successful counter-revolution affecting traffic would require a reorientation of a complex social pattern. Only a person bereft of reason would undertake to get state legislatures or the federal Congress to pass laws limiting drivers' licenses or raising gas taxes so that, as a consequence, the ratio of persons to cars would be what it was in 1910. The question for those who are radically dissatisfied with the basic premises of our present educational system to consider is the following: Was the transformation of 1905–1930 comparable to prohibition, or to the change in our methods of transportation? In short, is it or is it not a reversible social process?

For those who are at all familiar with the employment picture in the United States, to ask this question is to answer it. Nevertheless, I venture to remind the audience of a few facts of history which I find some contemporary critics of American public education sometimes seem to overlook. The first is the success of the movement to abolish child labor — a success which came only gradually to be sure. The second is the alteration of the attitude of labor leaders and management towards the employment of young people. The third is the continuous change in the nature of the demand for labor, a constant increase in the ratio of skilled to unskilled jobs. The fourth is the disappearance of the apprentice system as it existed in 1900 and still exists on the Continent of Europe. Taking the country as a whole, we find in 1910 that thirty percent of the youth fourteen and fifteen years of age were employed; by 1930 the figure had dropped to nine percent. For the sixteen- and seventeen-year-olds, the employment figure for 1910 was sixty-six percent; by 1930 it had dropped to thirty-two percent. The school enrollment of both groups had correspondingly increased.

To be sure, it was only in the days of the New Deal that national laws regulating child labor were passed that were not subsequently declared unconstitutional (the Walsh-Healy Public Contracts Act of 1936 and the Fair Labor Standards

Act of 1938). But in many heavily industrialized states, the new pattern had been established before Franklin Roosevelt took office. One has only to contrast the present European and American practices in the teaching of skilled mechanics to see what happened in this country in this century. In Germany, today, those who are to become skilled workers in metal start their apprentice work at age fifteen in a school run by a large industrial concern; they also attend a few hours each week a continuation school run by the state. In the United States, in some communities, the first year of apprentice work may be anticipated by vocational courses in grades eleven and twelve (under the Smith-Hughes Act) either in a vocational high school or a widely comprehensive high school. But apprentice training on the job rarely starts before a boy is seventeen or eighteen years of age.

Let me make it plain that in stressing the alteration in the employment scene I do not mean to imply that the educators had no influence on the transformation of the high school. The true interpretation of the revolutionary transformation of secondary education lies between the two extremes I earlier depicted. Professors of education and public school administrators were in part responsible for the changes which occurred. But so, too, were labor leaders, the humanitarian reformers seeking to abolish child labor, certain industrialists, and the innovating engineers who were altering the nature of industrial processes. So, too, in fact, were professors of the liberal arts who, when they saw the population of the public high schools altering, decided to leave the study of the new pedagogic problems to the professors of education.[1] No one could attempt to assay the relative contributions made by the professional educators acting directly on the content of the high school curriculum and the other group — labor leaders, humanitarian reformers — whose ideas and actions changed the framework within which the high school teachers had to operate. Chronologically, the two groups were simultaneous in their actions; as each decade passed, the results of their efforts reinforced each other.

As evidence in support of my somewhat dogmatic assertions about the changes in the composition of the high school student body, let me quote from an influential educator who was writing in 1917 — a year which falls halfway in the revolutionary period 1905–1930. The educator I have in mind is Alexander Inglis, in whose memory the annual lecture which I have the honor of giving this evening was established. In his *Principles of Secondary Education*, published in 1918, Professor Inglis writes about the "noteworthy changes [which] have taken place in the secondary school population." This population, he declares, has changed in the course of twenty-five years from "a roughly homogeneous group of those designed for the higher walks of life to a highly heterogeneous group of pupils destined to enter all sorts of occupations." [2] The causes of the change, which is referred to more than once in the volume, were primarily social and economic. But on one important point it seems clear that the educational reformers (of whom Inglis was an outstanding leader) had already had influence on the composition of the student body of the high schools and soon would have still more. A decade earlier, it had been widely accepted practice to restrict admission to a four-year high school to those who had satisfactorily completed the work of the first eight grades. As a consequence of this practice, a considerable number of students were repeating the work of the lower grades, and not a few were leaving school without even having entered high school. With the introduction of the junior high school, which was taking place at the time Professor Inglis wrote, rigid separation of the high school from the lower grades was broken down. Furthermore, promotion by subject, rather than by grades, was being advocated. One judges that, by 1917, it was far less common to find a sizeable fraction of the fifteen-year-olds in grade eight or lower. Just how widely what is now called "social promotion" had been adopted, I cannot say, and Professor Inglis' recommendation cannot be so classified. But it seems probable that an educational reform designed to correct a situation that found some young people two or three years older than their classmates had increased the heterogeneity of the high school population.[3]

Reading Professor Inglis' volume in the light of what has happened since was to me a fascinating experience. One saw a revolution through the eyes of a revolutionary, one might almost say, or at least a reform through the eyes of a reformer and his own appraisal of the social changes that made imperative the pedagogic reforms he was promoting. But, in addition, one reads an account of a process which was still going on and learns what the progressive educators at the time of World War I were predicting about the future. Reading the 1918 Report of the NEA Commission on the Reorganization of Secondary Education affords something like the same experience, but, since the Report is brief, the argumentation is kept to a minimum. Professor Inglis was a member of the NEA Commission and, I judge, an influential member. Certainly his book and the Report agree on all essential points.

The NEA Report to which I have been referring is generally known by its title, *Cardinal*

Principles of Secondary Education. There seems no doubt it has had, and still continues to have, a profound influence on the way public school people have formulated their problems and endeavored to explain to the public what they were accomplishing. Those who are primarily interested in the formulation of educational principles and pedagogic theories have centered their attention on the cardinal principles themselves. Such people are concerned to trace the influence of the progressive movement in education, which had started in the 1890's, on the principles and their elaboration by the NEA Commission.[4] The mood in which I am examining the transformation of the high school is one which, as I explained at the outset, is not congenial to educational theorizing. So, I may be forgiven if I skip over a large segment of the orthodox treatment of American educational history with only a single comment on the role of progressive education in the revolution with which I am concerned this evening. As I read the NEA Report, Professor Inglis' volume, and the writings of John Dewey before 1920, I am struck with the way the new ideas fit the new problems as a key fits a lock. Confronted with a "heterogeneous high school population destined to enter all sorts of occupations," high school teachers and administrators and professors of education needed some justification for a complete overhauling of a high school curriculum originally designed for a homogeneous student body. The progressives with their emphasis on the child, "on learning by doing," on democracy and on citizenship, and with their attack on the arguments used to support a classical curriculum, were bringing up just the sort of *new* ideas that were sorely needed. After closing John Dewey's volume, *Democracy and Education*, I had the feeling that, like the Austro-Hungarian Empire of the nineteenth century, if John Dewey hadn't existed, he would have had to be invented. In a sense, perhaps he was, or at least his doctrines were shaped by the school people with whom he talked and worked.

I have touched so far only on how the past and current scene appeared to Inglis and his colleagues — what I might call the first half of the transformation. Let us now examine their views about the future. It seems quite evident that they failed to realize in 1918 how rapidly the change in the high school population was taking place and how far it would go within another decade. At the time they were writing, the number who left school after completing only grades seven or eight was still large. The NEA Commission says of such pupils that their needs cannot be neglected, "nor can we expect in the near future that all pupils will be able to complete the secondary school as full-time students." [5] Inglis estimates, conservatively, that more than a million children were leaving school above grade six, and he goes on to state: "Compared with this the number of those completing the secondary school course . . . is insignificant." [6] One of the most compelling arguments for the junior high school (grades seven to nine inclusive), as presented by Inglis, was the need for giving those who left school before entering grade ten some of the educational experiences hitherto reserved for high school youth.[7]

The establishment of junior high schools with at least the beginnings of a high school curriculum was one answer to the problem presented by the numbers who were leaving school after reaching age fourteen. But Professor Inglis, and presumably the other educators in his company, wanted to do far more than cope with the existing situation. And here we meet the reforming zeal of the educator and recognize it as one, but only one, of the factors in the process which transformed the high school. The NEA Commission, arguing that secondary education was essential for *all* youth, made the following specific recommendation: "*Consequently this Commission holds that education should be so reorganized that every normal boy and girl will be encouraged to re-*

main in school to the age of 18 on full time if possible, other wise on part time." [8]

There are two points of interest about this recommendation. First, it appears inconsistent with one set of arguments in favor of the junior high school — the arguments based on the large proportion of pupils leaving school after reaching age fourteen. Second, it envisages part-time education as as alternative to full-time education. As to the first point, I think it clear that the writers of the Report feared that the raising of the school-leaving age would be a long slow process, and consequently it would be many decades before a large proportion of the sixteen- and seventeen-year-olds would be going to school. And they might well have been right, if the social and economic forces had been different. Actually, the raising of the school-leaving age in many states followed the change in the pattern of school attendance of a majority of the youth.

The second point requires a more lengthy comment. The possibility of part-time education by means of continuation schools was clearly very much in Professor Inglis' mind. He writes of the continuation school "so neglected in American education" and pleads that it be "given its legitimate and necessary place in coordination with the junior and senior high schools." [9] The Commission is quite specific about the need for such schools, and in a recommendation which is rarely remembered nowadays, the authors express themselves as follows: *"Consequently, this commission recommends the enactment of legislation whereby all young persons up to the age of 18, whether employed or not, shall be required to attend the secondary school not less than eight hours in each week that the schools are in session."* [10]

The Commission admits in the next paragraph that it may be impracticable at the outset "to require such part-time attendance beyond the age of sixteen or seventeen," but maintains that eventually the period must be extended to eighteen. Furthermore, the Commission states that to make the "part-time schooling effective" it must be adapted to the needs of the pupils. And in order to develop "a sense of common interest and social solidarity" with those who are full-time students, the instruction should be given in the comprehensive high school rather than in separate continuation schools which "is the custom in less democratic societies." [11]

This last is clearly a reference to Germany. And what is envisaged for the United States in this section of the Report is only a modification of the German practice of that day which, by the way, is still in operation. In Germany, then as now, part-time education begins at fourteen and is completed at sixteen; the formal instruction is given in special continuation schools. The Commission hoped that in the United States part-time education would be continued till age eighteen and provided in the same school which was accommodating those who desired full-time education through grade twelve. In other words, the comprehensive high school would enroll part-time as well as full-time students. Neither Professor Inglis nor the Commission prophesied as to what fraction of the youth would be enrolled part time and what fraction full time.

Let us see what actually happened in one large heavily industrialized state, New York. In 1919, the legislature enacted a law which required attendance of employed youth over fourteen and up to eighteen years of age in continuation schools for at least four hours a week during the day for thirty-six weeks and further required the establishment of such schools in districts of more than 5,000 in population. The law provided for the gradual development of a continuation school system to be started in September 1920 and to reach full capacity by September 1925. Contrary to the recommendation of the NEA Commission, the part-time students were cared for in separate schools of which fifteen were eventually established in New York City alone. The number registered in the continuation schools of the entire state rose steadily from 30,236 in 1921 to a peak

of 168,377 in 1928; of these 131,022 were enrolled in New York City continuation schools.
At this time, something like twenty percent of
the age group fourteen to seventeen in New York
State were enrolled in a continuation school for
part-time education. During the same period
(1921 to 1928), full-time enrollment in grades
nine to twelve was also rising rapidly; some
270,000 more pupils were enrolled at the end of
the period than at the beginning. (In these eight
years, the population, age fourteen to seventeen,
increased only by about 95,000.) In short, by
1928 about half the youth of New York were in
school full time; about twenty percent in school
on a part-time basis.[12]

I cannot help speculating what would have
been the course of American secondary education if the depression had not occurred or had
taken place a decade later. The pattern of secondary education had been transformed before
the depression; this fact is perfectly clear. When
it came to a choice between part-time and full-
time school attendance, many youth preferred the
latter. It would be a great error to assume that,
even in New York State, anything closely re-
sembling the German pattern of vocational education had been established. Furthermore, I am
told that vocational as well as academic work was
offered in the separate continuation schools set

up in the larger cities of New York. There is no evidence that the employment opportunities were of the apprentice type supported by industry, as would be the case in Germany.

But the part-time enrollment fell during the depression years, first slowly and then rapidly — from a peak of 168,000 in 1928 to 105,000 in 1933 and to about 30,000 just before World War II.[13] At first sight this swift decline in numbers would seem to show that the great depression had killed the continuation schools in New York. But a closer examination of the facts reveals that what actually happened was a transformation of the separate continuation schools into separate full-time vocational schools. The evidence in the case of New York is clear. Presumably, the situation was not very different in the other states which, in the 1920's, had also established continuation schools. In New York, the 1919 law had provided that, while employed youth were required to study only four hours a week, unemployed boys and girls had to study a minimum of twenty. Therefore, as employment opportunities declined, more and more young people were forced by law to lengthen their school attendance to at least twenty hours a week. As a matter of fact, many elected to do more and became essentially full-time students. In New York City, the school authorities, recognizing what had

happened, officially converted the separate continuation schools into separate vocational schools
which became a firmly established part of the
educational structure. These schools maintain a
part-time continuation unit in which a few students are enrolled even at the present time.

The short-lived experiment of continuation
schools on a large scale was a purely American
attempt to answer questions that are still with us.
How can you satisfy the youth who have little
academic ability and whose interests lie in the
direction of getting a job and developing a
manual skill? How can you at the same time provide a general academic education for this type
of student through twelve grades (or at least
eleven) and at the same time prevent boredom
and frustration? The continuation day school was
one answer, though only four hours of formal instruction a week hardly satisfies our present idea
of the amount of time which should be devoted
to general education.

Another answer was in process of formulation
just at the time the NEA Commission reported.
This answer was to keep all youth in high school
full time through grade twelve and provide the
facilities and instruction for meaningful vocational education. And to forward this solution,
the United States Congress passed the Smith-
Hughes Act in 1917, appropriating money for

vocational education. In his book, Professor Inglis indicated that he had great expectations for vocational education with the passage of the Smith-Hughes Act. (He was writing in 1917, remember.) It is clear that he and the members of the NEA Commission favored the development of vocational education within the comprehensive high school instead of in separate vocational schools. And such a development did take place in the next twenty years in many localities in many states. In three states — Massachusetts, Connecticut, and Wisconsin — the state authorities concerned with vocational education were unwilling to trust the principals of the general high school. It was thought that the schools would be so academic in their orientation as not to give the vocational courses a fair chance. It was argued that only in separate vocational high schools could the federal and state funds be used to advantage for the education of boys in the skills of trade and industry. In New York City, as I have already pointed out, the fifteen continuation schools turned into vocational schools in the 1930's. A similar pattern seems to have developed in the large cities throughout the country.

This is not the time or the place for me to discuss the advantages and disadvantages of the separate vocational school. There are only a few cities where the issue now arises. What I should like to point out is how in the 1920's two rival methods of handling one educational problem were developed with the blessing of the professional educators and how the depression essentially destroyed one method — the continuation school — and thereby favored the other — vocational education at the secondary level.[14] Of course, the two rival methods were different in their pedagogic content. Under the continuation school plan the learning of a skilled trade did not take place in school and only took place at all if suitable employment opportunity was open. The other method involved the student's devoting half his time in school in grades eleven and twelve to vocational work.

The victory of vocational education at the secondary level left unsolved the problem of the very slow readers. Quite rightly, vocational directors today refuse to have the educational facilities under their direction used as dumping grounds for those of very low academic ability. Under the continuation school plan, these students would have been better cared for, provided suitable employment was available and provided the required schooling occupied at least one-half the school day — two large provisos, I must admit. Yet I see signs of a movement in the direction of some such scheme. I talked to a principal not long ago who arranged to have students experiencing great difficulty with their formal studies (in part because of lack of interest) come to school only in the mornings; in the afternoons they had a part-time job which was satisfactory.[15] What had been worked out in this particular school for a few students was quite similar to the type of part-time education envisaged by the NEA Commission in 1918. For you will recall, the Commission recommended that the continuation classes be part of a comprehensive high school and *not* be offered in separate schools. Continuation schools and continuation classes still exist in some states and some cities but play a very minor role in the entire educational process. The amazing popularity of the continuation schools in New York in the 1920's has been almost entirely forgotten. There is no possibility of reverting to this type of education for any large numbers. I cannot help wondering, however, whether for certain kinds of pupils part-time education may not be the answer, assuming that suitable employment opportunities are available and that the boy or girl is sixteen years of age or older.

It is getting late and it is time I attempted a summary of my story. For purposes of exposition, I have broken the revolutionary transformation of the high school which occurred between

1905 and 1930 into two parts. By so doing, I was able to see how the transformation looked to the reformers who were writing in 1918 at the midway point. Clearly, the total process is irreversible, though in two details — vocational education and the education of those who have great difficulty with their studies — the pattern is far from firm. To my mind, in these areas further searching examination is required. But for the examination to be profitable it must be city by city and town by town. I should start by questioning the dogma one often hears that all the youth, irrespective of academic ability and interest, should complete grade twelve. Above all, the relation of education to employment of youth sixteen and over must be constantly kept in mind.

I have said the evidence is clear that we cannot turn the educational clock backwards; we cannot return to the situation of 1900 or even 1910. This is so because of complex social and economic changes in the United States which have created a society unlike any other in the world. Yet I do not want to close on what may appear to be an economic deterministic note. The reforming educators played their part in the whole transformation; to some degree they guided the boat, even if it was propelled by a power over which they had no control. Let me remind you of the reforming spirit which characterized the

United States in the first two decades of this century. Education was believed in as though it were a newly discovered magic process. Presidents of colleges clinging to a classical pattern of education proclaimed its virtues as loudly as reformers like John Dewey. Such faith was in accord with the spirit of the day. American public opinion was predominantly in an optimistic humanitarian mood. One has only to remember the calls to political action of the elder LaFollette and Theodore Roosevelt to see why the radical transformation of the high school population was almost taken for granted by those who were American leaders just before World War I. Perhaps it would be fair to say that the changes in secondary education I have been discussing were the consequence of the harmonious reinforcement of a variety of forward moving currents in the history of this country — that the high schools of the 1930's (which followed essentially the same educational pattern as do high schools of today) were the creation of a prolonged surge of sentiment of the American people. I should call it a surge of noble sentiment. But my use of the adjective may only betray the fact that I was not only alive, but young, in the period when the waves of hope for humanity were running high.

I must confess, as I have reviewed the educational history of that period, I find my faith and optimism returning. So I venture to close this Inglis Lecture with a prophecy. If the free world survives the perils that now confront it, I believe historians in the year 2059 will regard the American experiment in democracy as a great and successful adventure of the human race. Furthermore, as an essential part of this adventure — indeed, as the basic element in the twentieth century — they will praise the radical transformation of America's treatment of its children and of its youth. They will regard the American high school, as it was perfected by the end of the twentieth century, as not only one of the finest products of democracy, but as a continuing insurance for the preservation of the vitality of a society of free men.

NOTES

1. In 1910, the older eastern colleges occupied a relatively far more important position than they do today, in the fields of both scholarship and athletics. The fact that the student body of these institutions was then predominantly recruited from private schools explains why the faculties were but little concerned with the new problems of the public schools. Furthermore, one might assume that in 1910 the majority of students in the public schools of eastern cities who wished to go to college could enroll in specialized academic schools like the Boston Latin School. See Alexander Inglis, *Principles of Secondary Education* (Boston: Houghton Mifflin, 1918), p. 197, for a table showing the change in private and public high school enrollments 1889 to 1915. The public school figures jumped from sixty-eight to ninety percent of those attending high school.

For a penetrating analysis of the influence of such humanitarian groups as the settlement workers in the education field, see Lawrence A. Cremin, "The Progressive Movement in American Education: A Perspective," *Harvard Education Review*, Vol. XXVII, No. 4, Fall, 1957. On page 260 Professor Cremin writes: "In reality, school reform and municipal reform were frequently if not always facets of the same progressive movement; to understand them as such is to expand significantly our comprehension of progressivism both in politics and in education."

Another factor which helps to explain the educational transformation of 1905–1930 is the great increase in non-English-speaking immigration during the last quarter of the nineteenth century and continuing into the first quarter of the present century. Whereas less than sixty percent of the foreign-born population of the United States was non-English-speaking in 1890, twenty years later almost three quarters of this group were so classified. The secondary school faced many important problems arising out of this immigration, "involving a longer period of education and an education which should aim definitely toward the integration of large groups of different forms of social heredity." (Inglis, p. 98)

2. Inglis, p. 577. On p. 146, he writes: "During the last decade of the nineteenth century and the beginning of the present century there has been a marked increase in the attendance in the public secondary school of pupils who were not destined for higher education." On p. 370, he writes: "As long as pupils receiving the benefits of secondary education were drawn from classes whose vocations were almost entirely the higher professions, involving vocational education in higher institutions, the directly vocational aim in the secondary school was subordinated to other aims except in so far as preparation for higher institutions might be conceived

as involving indirect contribution to a vocational aim. With the extension of the benefits of secondary education to the non-professional classes greater importance has necessarily been attached to the economic-vocational aim."

On p. 119, Inglis writes: "The great increase in the number of secondary school pupils is in part the result and in part the cause of the extension of the curricula to meet the diversified needs of different groups of pupils . . . Pupils of types not attending the secondary school before 1890 now are enrolled in large numbers."

In 1913, the National Education Association appointed a Commission on the Reorganization of Secondary Education. This Commission issued thirteen separate reports, the most well-known of which was entitled *Cardinal Principles of Secondary Education* (Bulletin 1918, No. 35, Department of the Interior, Bureau of Education, Government Printing Office). On p. 8, the authors state: "In the past 25 years there have been marked changes in the secondary school population of the United States. The number of pupils has increased, according to Federal returns, from one for every 210 of the total population in 1889–90, to one for every 121 in 1899–1900, to one for every 89 in 1909–10, and to one for every 73 of the estimated total population in 1914–15. The character of the secondary school population has been modified by the entrance of large numbers of pupils of widely varying capacities, aptitudes, social heredity, and destinies in life."

3. Inglis, p. 77, Table XXV. Though the median age of 949 pupils entering New York City public high schools in 1906 was fourteen years, six months, twenty percent were a year or more older.

On p. 7, Table III, Inglis gives the data for six cities showing that the twelve-year-olds were distributed in considerable numbers over grades five, six, and seven and as many as twenty-three percent of the sixteen-year-olds still in school were enrolled in grades eight or lower.

On p. 276, Inglis writes, "The large number of over-age pupils found in the elementary school raises some serious questions concerning methods of promotion in the later grades of that school . . . the practice, hitherto obtaining, of retaining pupils chronologically, physiologically, and socially mature in the lower grades of the school system and making the complete accomplishment of prescribed amounts of elementary-school work the sole criterion for the admission of pupils to other forms of education is a practice harmful both to the school and to the pupils."

Inglis, pp. 123–127, discusses retardation and acceleration and at the end of the discussion concludes: "It would appear that the public secondary school is ill-adapted both to the needs of the duller pupil and the needs of the brighter pupil."

On p. 294 and p. 696, Inglis writes of "promotion of pupils by subjects rather than by grades."

The NEA Commission (*op. cit.*), p. 19. "Admission to high school is now, as a rule, based upon the completion of a prescribed amount of academic work. As a result many over-age pupils either leave school altogether or are retained in the elementary school when they are no longer deriving much benefit from its instruction . . . *Consequently we recommend that secondary schools admit, and provide suitable instruction for, all pupils who are in any respect so mature that they would derive more benefit from the secondary school than from the elementary school.*" (Italics in the original.)

4. Lawrence A. Cremin's "The Revolution in American Secondary Education, 1893–1910," *Teachers College Record*, March 1955, is an excellent account of the progressive movement and its effect on the high school curriculum.

5. NEA Commission, *op. cit.*, p. 8.

6. Inglis, p. 576.

7. Inglis, pp. 293–295, devotes four paragraphs to the purposes of the junior high school which was at that time a very new invention. Included are the arguments given by the NEA Commission (*op. cit.*, pp. 17–19) which emphasized the need in grades seven, eight, and nine for a "pupil to explore his own aptitudes and to make at least provisional choice of the kinds of work to which he will devote himself." The Commission goes on to say (p. 19): "In the junior high school there should be the gradual introduction of departmental instruction, some choice of subjects under guidance, promotion by subjects,

pre-vocational courses, and a social organization that calls forth initiative and develops the sense of personal responsibility for the welfare of the group."

The basic need for the junior high school as presented by Inglis seems to be tied to the fact to which he repeatedly returns, namely, the large number of youth who never reach even grade nine. Thus, he writes (p. 295): "If all pupils were destined to continue in school throughout the full twelve-year course and if the exigencies of administration made it possible, it would be advisable to have one undivided system consisting of grades one to twelve. Neither of those assumptions hold, however, and it is probable that they never can hold." And on pp. 694–695, again Inglis states: "It is important that some of the phases of secondary education be operative before the majority of pupils leave school."

The curricula of the junior high school suggested by Inglis (pp. 685–687) are most interesting, required subjects (constants) occupying a decreasing amount of time as one passes from grade seven to nine. Variables (electives) include foreign languages beginning in grade seven. The choice between algebra and commercial arithmetic is to be made in grade eight.

8. NEA Commission, *op. cit.*, p. 30. (Italics in the original.)

9. Inglis, p. 707.

10. NEA Commission, *op. cit.*, p. 31. (Italics in the original.)

11. *Loc. cit.*

12. The statistics here quoted and much valuable information about the continuation school in New York State were kindly supplied by Dr. Joseph R. Strobel, Assistant Commissioner for Instructional Services of the New York State Education Department. Also, Franklin J. Keller's *Day Schools for Young Workers* (New York and London: The Century Company, 1924) and *The Changing Pattern of Continuation School Education In New York City; An Appraisal and a Prognosis*, a report prepared by a sub-committee of the Vocational High School Planning Committee, December 1956, were consulted.

13. That the depression was responsible for the rapid falling off in the registration in the part-time continuation schools in New York State is made evident by the following statistics concerning enrollment:

1927	158,603	1932	141,626
1928	168,377	1933	104,987
1929	164,905	1934	74,949
1930	161,201	1935	54,232
1931	149,856	1936	56,250

In 1935, the legislature made attendance at school *full time* compulsory until sixteen, and no full-time employment certificates could be issued to those under sixteen, effective September 1, 1936. The sixteen-year-olds who had not graduated from high school were required to attend continuation school. Enrollments in part-time continuation schools and classes fell steadily to a low of 15,497 in 1942. In 1940, the law was again amended requiring continuation schools only in cities of over 400,000 population and districts having 1,000 minors aged sixteen who were obliged to attend such schools. In 1958, only three cities in New York State offered continuation courses: Buffalo, New York City, and Troy, the last on a voluntary basis. The enrollments were: New York City 18,787, Buffalo 500, Troy 151. It is correct to say that the continuation school has essentially disappeared.

14. Professor Inglis' chapter on "Practical and Vocational Arts" is interesting in view of what has happened since. Among the factors affecting the need for vocational instruction in the high schools, he mentions the following (p. 595): "The constantly increasing division of labor has tended to prevent those engaging in industrial activities from securing in industry itself broad training in the trades and crafts . . . The apprentice system which formerly afforded valuable industrial education has tended to disappear, only 118,964 apprentices being accounted for in the entire country in the reports of the 1910 census . . . The increased mobility of labor has tended to discourage attempts on the part of employers to train a body of broadly expert workmen and workwomen who may leave his employ at any moment after he has gone to the expense of their industrial education."

15. The difference between such an arrangement and the work experience program to be found in many schools is worth consideration. Under the work experience programs, a teacher or director is responsible for both the work in school and some supervision for the work done on the job. Only students with at least average academic ability are encouraged (or usually allowed) to enroll. The number of places is highly limited because only a relatively few suitable openings are available in the community; employment opportunities not tied into an educational program are usually far greater. More high schools might well examine, it seems to me, the possibility of finding part-time jobs for certain types of students sixteen years of age or over, even if the employment is in no way related to the program of studies in the school.